Seven days in Fiji

By Steve Glines

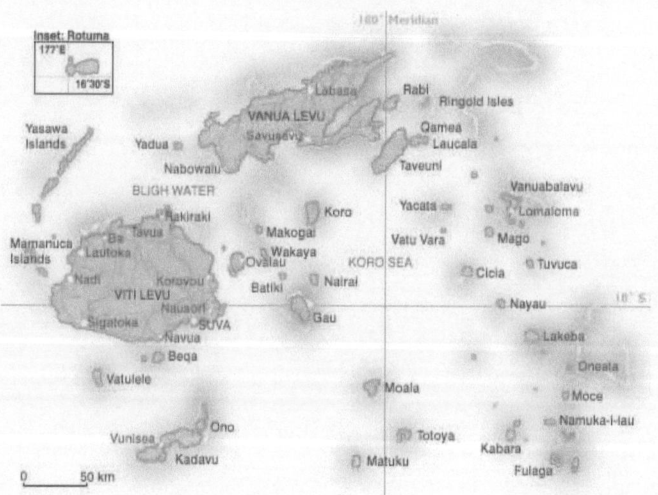

Seven Days in Fiji

ISBN 978-1-4116-8649-6

To Suds Macklen
The smartest man I have ever met and who delayed his 90th birthday party so that I could finish this.

To Aruind Keshwal
My business partner in Fiji

Seven Days in Fiji

Table of Contents

Getting There

I have a seven-hour jet lag or is it 17 hours. I just got back from Fiji[i] and I'm not a happy person right now. Traveling used to be a grand experience. It's not anymore. When my dad went to China in the 1920's he didn't go for a week or so, he went for a year or so. The journey would begin with the family gathered at Grand Central Station in New York City to see my father off. He would have a private compartment in a Pullman car on the 20th Century Limited[ii] bound for Chicago. Half a dozen steamer trunks would be loaded into the baggage car with a large valise serving as a traveling wardrobe. In another bygone era my Grandfather would travel the world with a manservant but my Dad was a thoroughly modern 20th Century man, he traveled alone.

The trip to Chicago would take the entire night. Leaving at 6 in the evening, the 20th Century Limited wound its way up the Hudson River, crossing near Albany. From there the tracks paralleled the old Erie Canal through upstate New York, never stopping until it reached the suburbs of Chicago. With luck the trip would take a short 12 hours but bad weather or problems on the line could delay arrival by many hours. The last run of the 20th Century Limited was on December 2nd 1967, she was nine hours late. Layovers were not measured in hours but in days. A day or two layover was not a problem since it is likely that my Dad knew some business men he wanted to connect with on his way to the Orient. If there was a residential Harvard Club in Chicago in 1920 I'm sure he would have had his secretary book a room. If not there were other clubs and grand hotels available to accommodate him.

My Dad traveled with a portfolio of “letters of introduction” from various businessmen and bankers designed to gain access to and cash from various potentates along the way. One letter of introduction from the President of the Chemical, Corn Exchange Bank in New York City, dated 1927, and reads, “This letter is to introduce you to E. Stanley Glines. His credit is good in seven figures.” In 1927 my Dad could borrow a million dollars from anyone recognizing the signature of the bank president.

Trips like this were not the light business junkets we take today or the heavy progress of a wealthy prince across the interior. A business trip was a combination pitch to investors, a search for backers and the accumulation of the goods and services needed at the end of the line. One did not go across the country to shake hands as we do today. A business trip was a self-contained business that wheeled and dealed from one end of the world to the other and might involve dozens or hundreds of side deals on the way to the one BIG DEAL. My Dads first trip to China was a textbook example of an early 20th Century (or one might say late 19th Century) business trip. He was on his way to China for Stone and Webster Engineering in Boston to survey for a railroad to be built from Peking to Ulin Bator in Outer Mongolia. Along the way he agreed to export from China Chinese tea, and import into China a series of coin and money presses for the newly formed Imperial bank of China to which my Dad was credited as a founding partner. I think the

Bank of China was itself a side deal that allowed the financing of the railroad with local Chinese and British money.

After a night's rest and a day of shaking hands and explaining his mission my Dad would head back to the railroad for the long trip on the Overland Limited which left Chicago at 10:30 a.m. and arrived in San Francisco at 8:30 a.m. three days later.

Figure 1 Paintings by Howard Fogg - In 1917, the famous train is shown heading west past the spectacular cliffs of the Green River in Wyoming.

Once in San Francisco my Dad would again have looked up business acquaintances and exercised his *letters of introduction.* I do know from reading his journal of that first trip, that he spent considerable time in San Francisco before embarking for Shanghai. The manufacturing company that made the machinery for the San Francisco mint had been contracted as a part of a side deal to manufacture the machinery and presses for the Imperial Bank of China. My dad had to see that the equipment was packed and booked for shipment with him. This trip had begun to resemble an expedition. It reminded me of stories of Winston Churchill heading off to the Boar War with 12 trunks that included several hundred bottles of wine and spirits.

Somewhere in my dads journals he describes the journey aboard the passenger steamer leaving San Francisco for Shanghai. Along the way they stopped for a day in Honolulu Hawaii, Tokyo Japan and finally Shanghai, a journey of over 6,000 miles at an average of 12 knots. The math yields 20 days at sea but in reality this was a month long trip with days spent loading and unloading cargo, re-provisioning and coaling at every stop. There was some 1920's Hollywood starlet that was also traveling to China aboard the same ship and my dad spent considerable time in her company but my mother could never get my dad to admit they had an affair. Perhaps they didn't.

My dads business wasn't in Shanghai but rather in Peking and north to Ulan Bator in Outer Mongolia. It took him more than a month to get to Peking and another three to survey the tract between there and Ulan Bator for a railroad spur. Along the way he met and exchanged gun fire with bandits, discovered that he was smuggling guns in the crates he thought were printing presses, had a partner die in a sleeping bag next to him, had camel dung smeared all over his face as a cure for acute sunburn and met "Vinegar Joe" Stillwell in a bar that sounded like the intergalactic bar in the first Star

Wars movie. My dad and "Vinegar Joe" both tried to pay for their meals with cigar coupons. Both fled for their lives on camel back the next day when a marauding army of White Russian Cossacks sacked the city. This make me think that the Harry Flashman[iii] stories could very well have been a retelling of the life of some real non-fiction character.

Even though China in 1920 was as wild as any place on earth my dad made a good fortune on that business trip and made three more before 1940. Along the way he managed to meet everyone[iv] that was anyone in China from Sun Yat Sen, the founder of modern China, to Chiang Kai-shek and even Mao and Chou En-lai. He liked Sun, thought Chiang pompous and despised Mao as an uneducated buffoon but thought Chou En-lai was brilliant but unprincipled.

By these standards I did not make a business trip to Suva Fiji. My trip was not a business expedition; I flew in, taught a class for 40 hours then flew out. It was like a WWII bombing mission more than a business expedition. Like my fathers yearlong trips the minutia of the trip is what's interesting.

I don't think travel by itself is conducive to being creative. As far as I can remember Lord Byron is the only one who actually wrote anything of interest while traveling. I think he wrote a volume of poetry on his way out of England. That could have been Shelly. I can't remember. The point is that the act of traveling while inspirational is not conducive to actual production, at least not for me. Whenever I travel I bring my laptop and occasionally think about pulling it out. I never do. There are lots of opportunities to write or read. I have seen people reading or using their laptops while queued up to deposit their luggage at the check-in counter. I have seen people using their laptops for watching DVD's while waiting mindlessly in uncomfortable seats for airplanes to show up and, of course, I've seen people using laptops while on long flights from here to there. I can't do any of these things.

For me there is something acutely painful and, at the same time, compelling, about travel that will not allow me to read or write or watch a movie. On trips at night or when there is nothing interesting to see, like on long airplane rides, I go into hibernation. My pulse slows, my creative thought process is turned off and I drift in and out of sleep, a light torpor resembling sleep actually, and all except that portion of my brain that serves as my memory recording center is turned off.

The stupidity of the shoe bomber induced shoe X-Rays and the stealing of micro-penknives by brain dead security people don't phase me. I duly, or dully, comply and record the fact that I should be outraged in my memory. At best I shake my head and probably look a bit disgusted but I cannot recall uttering any actual verbal abuse. My actions are minimalistic. I know I have to take my laptop out of my bag so that it can be X-Rayed separately. If I were going to blow up an airplane it would be very easy but I have no inclination to do so and no access to Plastique. I take my laptop out, dump my keys, wallet, change, watch and jacket in the little bins provided, take my ticket (and boarding pass) in hand and walk through the metal detector without talking off my shoes. Taking shoes off is a major annoyance and putting them back on takes time. That only raises the anger level of those who have not yet learned to fall back into a stupor.

I don’t look like a shoe bomber and the unconscious mind of the security guards thank me for not slowing down the line. I walk through without protest. I carefully, deliberately and without rushing put my kit back together. My laptop goes back into the plastic bag I use for travel. That goes into my briefcase. My watch goes back on my wrist, keys, change and wallet go back into their appropriate pockets and my ticket and boarding pass back into the jacket pocket from whence it came. I put my jacket back on. I dust my self off, perform an accounting, then, if all is well, step away from the counter. My actions must incite a form of mental torture on the security guards watching me for while I am performing this slow ballet the line must come to a complete stop. I am deeply conscious of many eyes watching as I perform this deliberate but perfectly correct dance. They cannot say anything they are mesmerized.

I walk away from the X-Ray machine with all consciousness turned off save one small mental trigger: where is gate 32b? I find it, check my watch and set my mental timer for the required interval between now and when I expect the boarding announcement. That set I can go back into “the zone.” My timing is almost always perfect. During the period of languor I observe that most people are in the same state I am in, asleep or trying to amuse themselves. Into this latter category fall people chatting on cell phones, attempting to read and using laptops. Most people are used to multi-tasking with cell phones and the ones chatting with ephemeral friends are the only people fully engaged and animated. I notice that those trying to read never quite achieve the level of concentration I see in other public places. When people at the beach or in the library read there is almost a universal total absorption. This doesn't happen at the airport. I noticed that people using laptops at the airport fall into two categories. Those in the first category are people simply using their laptops as DVD players. These people are watching TV and, just as they would be at home, passively absorbing the contents of their tiny screen. I am at least moving my eyeball but am just as passively absorbing the contents of my field of vision. I am not sure who is being entertained the most.

The second class of laptop users are those trying to do something useful. Like those attempting to read they are fighting the inexorable boredom that sucks any and all creativity out of those waiting for a flight. I can tell who they are by the scowls and quiet curses they utter unconsciously and, usually, silently, just mouthing the invective. Try as they might to remain engaged in whatever is present on their screen they cannot as boredom sucks the light out of otherwise brilliant people. My eyes fixed on a woman who stared without the slightest hint of comprehension at the same page of the same text document for almost an hour. She was interrupted just when my mental timer went off and the "pre-boarding" announcement scratched over the barely comprehensible public address system.

The "pre-boarding" announcement is actually a boarding announcement, where they start boarding the young, the infirm and those taking care of the young and infirm. It's a boarding announcement, nothing "pre" about it. I'm not sure why it annoys me so much except that it is a gross misuse of the English language. For the next 20 minutes I actually have to be alert. I take inventory again, extract my boarding pass, reconfirm my seat number, 48d, and tune into the real boarding announcement. I've always loved the fact that they board 1st class passengers first. They get in their cushy leather seats that cost as much as 10 times what I pay, strap themselves in then have to sit and suffer the gawks and stares while the great unwashed masses in the back of the plane get on board and check them out. Some may enjoy this but if I were rich or famous I'd want to be the last one on board rather than be subjected to the scrutiny of hundreds of people I didn't know. I'll admit, every time I board an airplane I'll slow down and scan the faces of the first class passengers for someone famous. I've never seen anyone famous in first class but I am also sure I have stared blankly right into the face of someone I should know but didn't recognize. I'll bet the best paparazzi have walked right past someone famous in an airport without aiming a camera at them. Airports by design or accident are that numbing.

I find my seat, stow my carry on luggage in the overhead bins, lock my seatbelt and disengage. There is nothing, absolutely nothing I can do to affect the progress of this flight, my own life or career or the progress of civilization in general for the next six hours. My torpor is deeper now. I hear, without comprehension, the announcement about seatbelts and escape hatches (has anyone ever successfully evacuated an airplane by way of these hatches and slides?). I feel the plane being pushed away from the gate. I feel, more than hear, the engines being wound up. I feel the bumpy ride as we taxi to the end of the runway. I feel the acceleration as the plane forces its way down the runway. I semi-consciously estimate the speed, 70, 80, … 130, 140, 150, 160, 170 knots.

I can usually guess within a small fraction of a second the point where the pilot rotates the nose up and the front landing wheels rise from the pavement. With my eyes closed I can hear the difference more than feel it. When the plane rotates the lift on the wings suddenly increases dramatically and the instant this upwards thrust equals the weight of the plane we have liftoff. For most jets this rotation takes 2 – 3 seconds with the main wheels rising from the runway about ½ second into this rotation. For those who have never flown in a jet this moment must be terrifying. Five or six seconds after the wheels leave the pavement, a couple of seconds after the pilot has finished rotating the nose up, the main landing gear are retracted into the body of the plane with a "ta-thump, thump" sound loud enough bring me to full consciousness for a second or so. Then, depending on the jet, airline and pilot, the flaps and slots have to be retracted. The sound of flaps being retracted is a series of "whirr" sounds followed by another "ka-thump" when the flaps are fully stowed. Each retraction of the flaps is accompanied by a slight change in flight angle. My inner ear is more attuned to this change than my eye or ear. By the time the flaps are retracted the plane has gained enough altitude that my ears pop. Until your ears pop you become progressively deafer and deafer as the pressure on the inside of the eardrum presses out and the vibrations that power hearing become muted. The moment the pressure differential between inner and outer eat is equalized your hearing improves which is to say the sound inside the cabin suddenly becomes very loud.

This is the last time I am awake before landing six hours later. This time the sequence is in reverse. About half an hour before landing the plane begins its decent from about 30+ thousand feet. The decent is gradual and the pilot usually just pulls way back on the power. You can hear and feel the change in thrust and within a minute or so feel the change in cabin pressure. Most modern jets, specially older ones, leak air like a sieve so its hard to maintain a cabin pressure equal to 8,000 feet at 40,000 but that gets easier as the plane descends so your ears begin to pop as the plane passes 25,000. If you keep your eyes closed you can feel the air getting bumpier and thicker as the plane drops into the "teens."

The landing gear comes down first with a big thump. I'm still in a light torpor so I am just slightly more than recording of events. Having done this before I mentally match the current flight with past flights, looking for any deviation. The gear come down first, I reason, because the pilot needs an efficient air brake and the landing gear serve that purpose adequately, after all we have been descending at a relatively steep angle and must be going quite fast. When I've been able to observe the actual altitudes of jetliners (on the screens on the seat back in front of me) they seem to be ordered down in 2,000-foot decrements starting at 9,000 feet. Each decrement in altitude is accompanied by an extension of the trailing edge flaps and that “whirring” sound. At 5,000 feet we are cleared for landing. That’s when the pilot tells the flight attendants (I grew up calling them stewards and stewardesses) to have a seat. About this time the pilot realizes that he’s going to slow or is to low to make the runway and gooses the engine one last time. I am fully awake with my seat belt fastened (it never came unfastened), my tray table stowed and my seat back in the fully upright position. If we are going to crash this is when it will occur. I’ve crash-landed twice in my life and if I need to try to try to get out of this airplane via the hatches and shoots it will be in the next 10 minutes.

We hit harder than I expect, a crash, slam onto the runway at 200 knots. We shimmy in the 20 knot cross wind as the pilot, heart no doubt pumping hard, struggled to gain control in the 10 or so seconds he had to land this bird or go around again. We are on the ground and committed. The spoilers, which also serve as air brakes, are up killing lift and insuring that we stay on the ground and the engines are thrown in reverse. There are times when this breaking sequence has happened well before the pilot had full control of the plane on the ground. Those landings are scary and I always give the pilot, if he shows his face after that, a “way to go” thumbs up. I always get a sheepish grin.

All my crash landings were in the old Viscount and Vanguard turboprops that Air Canada used to fly. One of the crash landings occurred when we blew a tire as the pilot was trying to get control of the plane on the runway and after he had committed to landing. We spun out of control and right off the end of the runway and onto some grass. Nothing happened to us except some frayed nerves. After an inspection we were towed to the gate. I had a window seat for the second crash landing. We were at altitude when I noticed that the engine nearest to me was pouring oil out of the nacelle. I mentioned that to the "cabin attendant" who went running up to the pilot. The pilot or co-pilot came back to have a look then ran back forward and feathered the engine. By then the dripping oil was on fire and black smoke as well as oil was pouring out of the engine. I guess there was a fire extinguisher in the engine because the black smoke turned to white then ceased altogether. Still the pilot made a serious dive for the nearest airport. We landed with a fanfare of fire engines prepared to do battle with a major airplane crash. After inspection by the pilot and crew we were towed to the gate again.

Other than a landing hard enough to congratulate the pilot, this leg of my trip was uneventful. I dragged my baggage from the overhead compartment, exited the plane, and passed through the one-way doors of security. I was in LA. In six hours I would be on another plane bound for Fiji. Landings are always exhilarating and I am awake and searching for the Air Pacific counter, which turns out to be in another building.

While still awake I wander through the maze of shops and restaurants. If you are stuck in LAX the international terminal is the only place with food and or coffee or a place to sit. There are no homeless people at airports? Airports are too uncomfortable even for homeless people although I wonder if I'd even notice them. The designers of modern airports must have made a study of what people don't like. The chairs are very uncomfortable and impossible to sleep in. The décor resembles that of a modern industrial warehouse. The wall-to-wall carpeting used in all airports use must be made of Kevlar. Thousands of people walk on it every day yet ten years later it looks the same. I've seen people so tired or in deep enough hibernation to actually sleep on this stuff. I wonder how people actually work here?

Two hours till boarding time, I pass through the security check point again and again I don't take my shoes off and again the I can feel an unconscious thank you and again I fall into a trance. Four hundred of us all bound for Fiji board a giant 747; my seat is 87h, an aisle seat. Most of the people around me are not white Americans. I am asleep before we are pushed away from the gate. It has been years since I've flown in a 747. It is a very heavy aircraft. I am forced awake when my ears pop and the roar of the aircraft is suddenly apparent. I hear the pilot explain that we will be cruising at 30,000 feet and will drift up to 37 or perhaps even 39,000 feet as we consume jet fuel. I drift back to sleep.

Six or seven hundred miles into the Pacific Ocean it begins as a small bump, big enough to register an "oh!" Quiet … then another sharp thud. The pilot turns the "fasten seat belt" sign on and our six-hour rollercoaster ride begins. At 200 knots the bumps are relatively soft, like driving on a road in need of repaving. You can get airsick, carsick and seasick from this kind of motion. At 585 knots the same turbulence produces bumps that are sharp, hard and abrupt, like hitting a pothole at 45 miles per hour. It's harder to get airsick from this white-knuckle kind of motion, it's too abrupt, but is also hard for most people to sleep through it. I have learned to. I've been in enough bumpy flights to know that it's unlikely that the airplane will fall apart even if it feels like it should. I've also learned that if I keep my eyes closed I can actually enjoy the ride. When you keep your eyes closed you have to rely on your other senses to make up the difference in sensory intake. In the case of turbulence you must rely entirely on the motion detection of your inner ear. One difference between driving fast in a car and driving fast in an airplane is that the bumps are in 3D. Not only do you go up and down as you would in a car but you can be jolted from side to side just as hard. The hardest to take and the hardest to identify is that the airplane also pitches and yaws just as dramatically. One channel on the TV screen on the seat back in front of me continuously showed speed, altitude and a crude projection of position on a map of the world. The altitude and speed were updated every 5 seconds or so. The altitude of our aircraft changed as much as 50 feet and the speed as much as 80 knots during these 5-second updates. After watching about ten cycles I turned it off and fell back into the zone.

For me, in my lethargic state, the bumps, bangs and sways slowly blend in with the static noise of engines combined with air rushing past the fuselage at nearly 600 knots and human voices speaking quietly. I fall deeper into my torpor. One thought hits me. Whenever I've encountered this kind of turbulence over the continental US the pilots usually drop to a more comfortable altitude, which forces the plane to slow down. This makes the plane late, often hours late. You can't do that over the Pacific Ocean where the nearest landing strip might be several thousand miles away. Over the Pacific in a 747 you have to grin and bear it because to do otherwise would mean having to ditch the plane in the ocean a long way from wherever I want to be. Not being able to affect my situation, often a source of anxiety for others is a source of tranquility for me. I inherited that from my Dad who, it was said, could sleep anywhere under any circumstances.

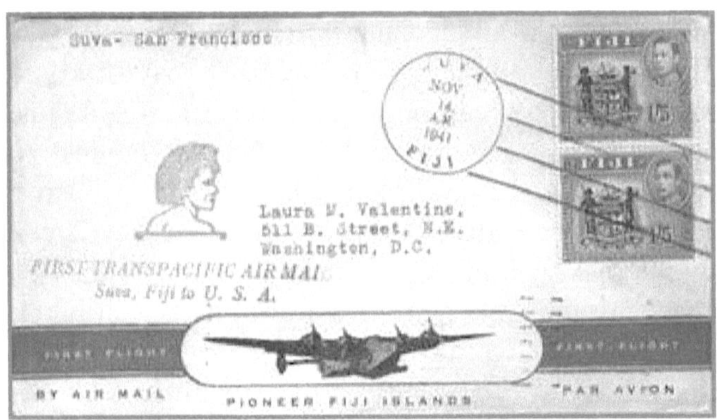

In Fiji at last

Landing in Nadi, Fiji was disappointment. It was normal but as soon as I walked across the threshold of the aircraft door and into the sunshine and warm tropical air I knew I was in a different place. That was my first impression of Fiji and when I turned around to look at the enormous aircraft I had just exited from I caught my first glimpse of the Nadi Mountains. They are rugged, sharp and distinct from any I have seen in North America.

Fiji is part of the Pacific Ocean's "Ring of Fire," a large collection of current and extinct volcanoes. Think of Fiji as Hawaii's southern brother. Fiji is a continental island that rests on its own plate. The oldest rocks in Fiji are about 40,000,000 years old. The island nation is made up of some 300 islands (at high tide) scattered over a small corner of the South Pacific. The higher islands are mostly made of basalt while the smaller atolls of reef formed limestone. The basalt, unlike the granite of New England, is relatively soft and porous. Weathering by wind and rain has given them a sharper, more vertical edge than the more rounded slopes we are used to in the north east coast of North America. Most of the islands of the south Pacific have this same geological look and feel. Tahiti, for example has a similar geological structure.

The island of Viti Levu, the main island in Fiji, is surprisingly large, about 100 miles (160 km) in diameter at its widest spot. To get to Suva, where I was going on business was 200 km (125 miles) by car but the company I was working for had made arrangements for me to fly to the airport nearest Suva at Nausori. The airport at Nadi is like every other international airport in the world. People speak English, the signs are in English and the Duty Free shops has the same overpriced merchandise found in *any* Duty Free shop *anywhere* in the world. The Nadi airport is not Fiji.

I had a window seat for the uneventful flight from Nadi to Nausori. From my seat I could see the tall ridges and valleys, roads and farmland, villages and dense jungle. The interior of the island is very thinly populated. The few roads I could see from my window were obviously dirt tracts leading along the valley bottom to small hamlets generally near a lake or on a river. As we descended into the Nausori airport we followed the Waimanu river as it grew from a relatively small stream to a large river navigable by fishing boats. The first thing that stuck me after landing at Nausori was how small the airport was and how quickly I could find a cab. My next surprise (and it should not have been a surprise) was that the Fijians drive on the wrong, that is British, side of the street.

The first five miles of my cab ride to Suva were more “white knuckle” than any part of the plane ride as we swerved around the traffic circles in the wrong direction. Because the major bridge over the river was being rebuilt we had to detour several miles around and through the construction. Like all construction projects there were a lot of workers supervising and a very few actually working. I mentioned this to my driver who remarked that this happened everywhere not just in Fiji. He was right of course but the number of laborers was astonishing. In a country like Fiji where the average income per capita is something like $3500 U.S. Dollars it’s cheaper to hire more laborers than it is to hire heavy machinery.

Fiji is very clean. I’m not sure why that surprised me but it is a lot cleaner than most cities in the US. I can walk down any street in America and find trash on the ground every few feet, you can walk down any street in Fiji and you won’t. It is enough of a difference to be startling. Then there is the smell. Fiji has a unique smell. It’s the combined smell of burning palm fronds and hardwood. Many people in Fiji don’t cook on stoves but rather on a small “hibachi” outdoors. This is true even if they have electricity and surprisingly it is also true inside Suva itself. There is the light scent of burning wood, slightly acrid but not unpleasant that hangs over the entire island.

As we drove into Suva we passed what my driver called “worker housing” or what we would call a housing project. This project had one-room apartments with cinderblock walls, tile floors, electricity and nothing else. Facilities with water, including a row of outhouses with flush toilets, were in a separate cluster away from the main cluster of buildings. There is no hot water here only cold. Hot water is what you make over a little electric stove inside your apartment or on a “hibachi” in the courtyard below. The good news is that it rarely gets above 85 degrees or below 72 degrees Fahrenheit so you don’t really need an air conditioner or any kind of heating. From this point of view Fiji is paradise. I’m not sure if there aren’t mosquitoes in Fiji or if there is an aggressive spraying program but I got bit only once and that was in Nadi not Suva.

Suva

Suva is a "created" city, invented by the British to serve as the national capital. The British invented much in Fiji. In 1882 Suva became the capital, 8 years after Fiji became a British Colony. Before the city was built the area looked like this:

SUVA IN VITI LEVU (THE FUTURE CAPITAL) WITH THE NAMOSI PEAKS.

The driver took me directly to the Suva Motor Inn. There are lots of hotels in Suva and mine was known to be a place ex-pat engineers are put up with little fuss. Except for the tile floors and funky oscillating fan attached to the ceiling my room could have been a room at any Motel 6 in America's southeast. I unpacked, took a short nap (Boston is 17 hours behind Fiji – so what time is my

head telling me?) then headed to the bar/restaurant for some coffee. Almost every hotel in the world has a swimming pool and some of the crummiest have "workout" rooms with broken equipment but creating spectacular swimming pools seems to be a matter of pride in the Fiji hospitality industry. The view from the bar at the Suva Motor Inn looks like this.

I was on the fourth floor. The shoot only went up to the second and no I didn't go down the shoot. In fact I never went in the pool. Here is another view stolen from their web site.

I **did** dip my big toe in the Pacific Ocean … once. At the end of the week I spent Friday night at a hotel in Nadi. It's pool looked like this with the obligatory waterfall.

I'll get back to Nadi later, right now I just got to Suva. The Suva Motor Inn is at the end of a very prestigious street, Gorrie Street. Prestigious in that the Fiji Red Cross and Fiji TV are all located on this relatively short, about 200 yards, mostly residential street. The end of Gorrie Street also marks the beginning of the nightly "red light" district. I didn't know what when I took off on a mission of discovery.

The Suva Motor Inn is right next to a small police station but if you walk in the other direction you pass the Fiji Red Cross (which was having a large reception – I was tempted to crash the party but didn't) and the headquarters of Fiji-TV. There are a few other mostly governmental buildings, a rundown hotel for tourists and some old rundown Fijian houses. At the end of the street, where the prostitutes congregate nightly, is one of the newer and more beautiful architectural sights in Suva. Suva is having a building boom, as is all of Fiji, and its often difficult to know what is going up or coming down.

To the right of this picture (point A in the map below) is a collection of small Fijian houses being demolished and to the left and down the street another 200 yards is the US embassy. From where I am standing to the entrance to the US embassy is the local nightly “combat zone.” Behind me at midday are government workers having lunch in the little park.

I love to walk. Where I live, in the far suburbs of Boston, there isn’t anywhere to walk to. The shortest “block” is about three miles. My first Saturday afternoon in Suva I walked for almost 4 hours … until I realized that I had very large blisters on both feet. I walked down Gorrie, turned left on Thurston St., passed the U.S. embassy and down to Victoria Parade, the main street in Suva. At this intersection I had a choice, turn right into the business district or left towards the Holiday Inn, the Botanical Gardens and the Presidential Palace. I went left on to Elizabeth Drive.

In case I haven't made it clear the British influence is everywhere and pervasive. English is the official language. The English Monarch is still considered the head of state and is represented on their currency and the British taste in food has regrettably infected this charming place. There are no three star restaurants in Suva but I was never tempted to eat at the local McDonalds. I found two of them, one in Suva and the other in Nadi.

Suva is making a break from its colonial past. Many of the old structures are being torn down or are being recycled into what we might call "mini-malls" full of hundreds of little shops. At the center of colonial Suva is the old and still impressive "Government Building." Today it mostly holds a museum and several courthouses. Right next to this old structure is Albert Park named after Price Albert, consort to Queen Victoria.

Figure 2 My neighborhood in Suva Fiji.

Albert Park is a wonderfully large open field. I can imagine parades of soldiers and horses marching up and down to impress the colonial governor, or bored colonial soldiers playing polo. Here is a postcard I found from the 1950's of the police band marching up Victoria Parade, the old colonial buildings are in the background as is Albert Park.

As I walked by Albert Park that first day I watched parts of a soccer game in one corner and a cricket came in the other. A week later they were still in the middle of that same game. I watched for an hour but couldn't devise the rules.

Cricket as seen by an American: Every once in a while a fellow would come running up to the pitchers mound and throw a ball. The fellow at the plate might or might not take a whack at the ball with his long thin paddle that serves as a bat. It seemed that every time he did take a whack at the ball he hit it but he rarely ever ran. This went on at a very slow pace seemingly forever until something happened and everyone went running around in some sort of organized melee. Over an hours time this happened twice but I never did figure out why or what happened to trigger the frenzy. The same game was still going on the following Thursday when I again stopped to watch. Cricket matches can run for weeks or even months.

I walked down Elizabeth Drive for about a mile, passed the Presidential Palace. Elizabeth Drive follows the coastline around the tip of Suva peninsula. Once you pass the old defunct Grand Pacific Hotel, Lawn Bowling Association and several soccer fields, the road runs along the seawall. In New England where we have tides that may be as high as ten or more feet we have seawalls that, in some places, are as high as 30 feet or more. In Fiji, where the tide is only a foot or so, the seawalls are no higher than three feet. Lots of people live within a few feet above sea level in Fiji. I love the ocean but there are two things that frighten me: Hurricanes (called cyclones in Fiji) and Tsunamis.

I walked along the seawall on Elizabeth Drive. On my left, as I walked out of town was the Presidential Palace

and a row of beautiful old shade trees. I don't know the species. Yes, in the background that is a hedgerow of flowering Hibiscuses

Here is the same area in 1954; the local army salutes the Queen when she arrived on her world tour.

Figure 3 Leaving the dais set up in Albert Park, the Queen closely followed by Ratu Sukuna, Fiji's most eminent indigenous leader at that time.

Elizabeth Drive is on the left, the seawall on the right:

Three days later and unknown to all an earthquake struck just north of the island and triggered a Tsunami warning[v]. The AP report reads:

Undersea Quake Strikes Near Fiji
SUVA, Fiji, Dec. 13, 2005

(AP) A powerful undersea earthquake struck near Fiji on Tuesday, geologists said, and officials issued a tsunami alert for the local area.

No damage or injuries have been reported.

The quake, with a preliminary magnitude of 6.3, occurred at 3:16 p.m. about 155 miles northeast of Vanua Levu, the main tourist spot in Fiji's chain of islands, at a depth of 18 miles, according to the U.S. Geological Survey.

Fiji, a chain of 322 islands, is

> southwest of Hawaii and due north of New Zealand, between Australia to the west and Tahiti to the east.
>
> The Hawaii-based Pacific Tsunami Warning Center issued a bulletin that said there was no Pacific-wide threat of a destructive tsunami, but that quakes of the size measured Tuesday could cause damaging local tsunamis.
>
> Nilesh Kumar, technical officer at Fiji's Mineral Resources Department, said there had been no reports of any tsunami and no reports from anywhere in Fiji of shakes being felt.
>
> Kumar said the department is maintaining a watch and is in communication with the warning center in Hawaii.
>
> The U.S. Geological Survey initially reported a second quake nearby, much deeper and with a magnitude of 6.8. But the survey removed the second quake from its Web site soon after details were posted.
>
> The survey says that when a large earthquake occurs it is common for seismological equipment in the area to incorrectly record multiple temblors, and that such glitches are quickly corrected on its Web site.

The Fiji authorities claim to have a good tsunami warning system in place but not a soul knew about it. In fact I didn't learn about it until I attempted to learn if the great tsunami of 2004 affected Fiji. It didn't. If the tsunami had materialized this beautiful view would have been ruined.

The tsunami didn't happen. I had blisters on my feet so I turned around and walked back towards town. On the way I tried to explore the Grand Pacific Hotel but was shooed away by a security guard. The old hulk looked like it had a fire. In its heyday it must have been magnificent. Today it just obstructs a beautiful view.

Figure 4 The Grand Pacific Hotel in 1920.

I took this picture looking past the old hulk from the other side of the building (B on the map). Until the opening of the Mocambo at Nadi and the Korolevu Beach Hotel in the 1950s, it was the only truly international - standard hotel in Fiji. In its time it was mentioned in the same breath as Singapore's famous Raffles Hotel.

The growing blisters on my feet colored my journey downtown but on a Saturday afternoon Suva is a bustling colorful city. There is a mall in downtown Suva where the escalators run up on the left and down on the right. It never dawned on me that escalators follow the same patterns that we use to drive cars. The mall is the only place where one finds purely western style shops. Most of the rest of Suva is filled with tiny shops selling clothing, shoes, CD's, cheap electronics and food. It's clear that the Indian population (more about that later) controls the local commerce. Indians own most of the stores.

There is a slightly seedy flavor about Suva that I love. It hasn't been sanitized the way most of America has. There is a sameness in the United States that makes Small City, Iowa look the same as Small City, New Jersey. Suva is different. Along Victoria Parade there are dozens of small shops, bars, restaurants and other shops, each with a crier selling the wares to be found inside. If you allow yourself to be ushered inside one of these stores you will be treated to a unique experience: one-on-one salesmanship with someone who actually knows the merchandise and is willing and eager to make a deal. Have you ever tried to find *any* salesmen in a "Big Box" store in the US?

I walked and walked until I found myself walking on the edges of my feet because the blisters prevented me from putting pressure on the ball of my feet. On my way back to the hotel I emptied my throw-a-way camera. Here is a small sample of the flavor of Suva Fiji:

Figure 5 This was taken from Location C on the map.

There are holdovers from the colonial period. They are charmed dinosaurs in a town rapidly forming its own, new, identity. First the old Melbourne Hotel in colonial days:

And now:

The first floor of this establishment has thousands of different cell phones, digital cameras and mp3 players from brands I've heard of and lots that I haven't. The top floor is one huge bar, the kind you would expect fights to break out in. On the way back out of town there was another colonial era building that housed a Chinese Restaurant and the South Pacific office of Greenpeace.

I stopped for dinner at the only Japanese restaurant I could find. It turned out to be a Samurai steakhouse. The food wasn't bad (it wasn't great either). I had Wasabi steak and some raw tuna, but the price was spectacular, $25 Fiji dollars for a good dinner and sake, about $15 US. My cook tried throwing his knife in the air like his counterpart all over the world but failed miserably almost skewering himself in the process. Then he tried juggling the industrial size salt and pepper shakers but dropped them. I was still amused. By the time I was done it was dark out.

Nightlife

I was tired and in spite of almost 15 hours sleep in the last 24, my head was telling me that it was 2 A.M. as it was in Boston. I headed back to the hotel wobbly walking on the edges of my feet so as not to put pressure on my growing blisters. Just as I turned up Gladstone Street, about a block from the U.S. embassy, a charming young lady, a Fijian, walked up to me and asked in a very proper (and disarming) British accent, "Sir, would you like some company tonight?" My immediate response was to feel flattered and apparently it showed for the young lady immediately grasped that I did not understand the nature of her proposition and added, "I could be yours for the evening for $50," she said with a lascivious wink. "Oh," I think I blurted out, "I'm sorry but I need to get a good night's sleep." I realized at that point exactly what I had said and its implication and must have blushed. The young lady laughed, and looked at me in an "I'm really sorry to have bothered you" kind of look, gently patted me on the back and said, "Well have a good night then Sir. Perhaps when you're feeling a bit more frisky you'll remember me."

It was still early Saturday night. The more enterprising streetwalkers hire cabs and troll the area looking for *johns,* leaning out of the window yelling, "Would you like some companyyyyyy" as they pass by. I had made it as far as the U.S. Embassy gate when I ran into a heard of the young ladies (and a few who were not). If I wasn't tired and a block from a bed and if I hadn't had a small bottle of *sake* in me I might have turned around and hailed a cab but I was tired and didn't really feel like breaking my stride so I pushed on. Almost immediately two young women took me by the arm asking if I'd like company. My brain was on autopilot. I didn't think, "How am I going to get out of this?" I didn't think "Oh no I might get robbed!" I didn't panic, as perhaps I should have being accosted by streetwalkers in a third world country. I think I smiled and grinned and said, "Do you take credit cards because none of the ATM's here seem to work?" Which was the truth.

One young lady immediately let go of my arm with a, "have a good evening Sir," but the other held on. She told me her name was something like "Lakota" and that I should be careful because many of the "girls" on the corner were "puftas," but that she was real. "What's that," I asked? "They are boys who think they are girls." She answered. She was still on my arm and I was beginning to think I might have a problem, "What do I do if she does take credit cards," I wondered? She walked me past the last of the "ladies" then patted me on the back and said, "Have a good night Sir, and remember me." How could I forget you? I doubt many streetwalkers anywhere are as polite or as entrepreneurial.

I had now been in Fiji about 12 hours. I was both tired and wired but If I was going to teach on Monday, which is why I was in Fiji, I needed to get my body and head into the Fiji time zone. I was in bed by 10:00 P.M. Fiji time. I put in a wakeup call for 6:30.

A Short History of Fiji,

as seen through the eyes of an itinerant American

Sundays in Fiji are a day of rest. Nominally almost half of the population of Fiji is Methodist. Historically the native chiefs would pledge themselves to Christianity while it was convenient but the lure of eating ones enemies constantly proved overwhelming to some. There are some alive today who knew someone who was a cannibal. See "The Whale Tooth[vi]," Jack London's fictionalized story of the killing (and eating) of missionary Thomas Baker. Civilization is a thin veneer at best and when a violent cultural tradition collides with modern pacifistic civilized ideals a cultural tradition of violence usually wins. I kept this in mind when I asked about Fiji's history and politics. I'm not an expert in Fiji history and what I am going to report is just an accounting of Fijian history as seen through my eyes.

Two characters of marginal repute unwillingly created modern Fiji. The first was an ambitious local chief named Ratu Seru Cakobau who was elected Fiji's first president in 1865 by a short lived confederacy of Chiefs. The second was a corrupt American Charge' d' Affairs who had an active import/export business. On the 4th of July 1849 he had a party with fireworks that ended up burning down his house and warehouse. The natives took advantage of the situation and looted what remained. Over the next twenty years, a bill for damages mounted and eventually the United States threatened annexation over the non-payment of the so-called debt, sending two sorties of warships over the years.

Political unrest and instability ensued, as western influence grew stronger. In 1871, with support of the approximately 2000 Europeans in Fiji, Cakobau was proclaimed king and a national government was formed in Levuka. His government, however, faced many problems and was not well received. To pay the American debt King Cakobau agreed to sell 200,000 Fijian acres to the Polynesia Company Ltd. which was consortium intending to grow cotton in Fiji. Things had started well enough when King Cakobau pledged the land which, unbeknown to the Polynesian Company's representatives in Fiji, were not wholly his to give. In return, the Company agreed to settle the indemnity levied by the United States government. An advanced payment ensured that his Fijian Majesty's problems with the United States government were over.

In early 1871, other problems were just beginning with investors showing concern about the land purchased for the Polynesia Company Ltd. Eventually, all the Company actually got for their money was approximately half the land it had originally been promised. Cakobau's feudal allies in the Suva Bay area, where some of the land in question lay, agreed to the transaction; but the chief of Rewa, the king's avowed enemy did not. Despite spirited onslaughts by the natives, by the middle of May 1871, eighteen of the forty allotments were ready for planting. What is now the town of Suva and a suburban reserve had been cleared as well.

King Cakobau actions were not well received by the Counsel of Chiefs and on October 10, 1874, after a meeting of the most powerful chiefs, Fiji was unilaterally ceded to the United Kingdom. This was the end of Ratu Seru Cakobau and the beginning of Pax Britannia in Fiji.

Fiji's first Governor under British rule was Sir Arthur Gordon. Sir Arthur's policies were to set the stage for much of the Fiji that exists today. In an effort to preserve the people and culture of Fiji, Sir Arthur forbade the sale of Fijian land to non-Fijians. He also instituted a system of limited native administration that allowed the native Fijians much say in their own affairs. A council of chiefs was formed to advise the government on matters pertaining to the native people.

Apparently the native Fijians were (and I can say still are) a happy lot and were not inclined to seek employment in the cotton and sugar cane fields. In order to provide cheap non-native labor for the plantations, the government looked to the crown colony of India. On 14 May 1879, the "Leonidas", the ship with the first indentured laborers from India, arrived in Fiji. Today, Indians ("FBI's," Fiji born Indians) make up over 45% of the population and clearly dominate the economy of the main island of Viti Levu.

If you think the United States has racial problems please visit Fiji. The tension between the Fiji and Indian population is palpable. As you enter the country there is a form that anyone traveling on a Fiji passport is required to fill out. It asks what race you belong to, the choices being: Fijian, Indian, other South Pacific Islanders, Caucasian and other. As you exit the country those of clearly Indian extraction are searched. As I stood in line expecting to be searched I received one of those, “I’m not here to search you, stupid,” looks from the Fijian inspector as she waved me though.

To the uneducated eye there isn’t all that much difference between Fijian and Indian people walking down the street. All have very dark skin, the Fijian people being mostly Melanesian rather than the lighter skinned Polynesian and the Indian people are mostly just as dark skinned. I made the mistake of mentioning my observation twice, once to a Fijian and once to an Indian. The difference, I was told, are that the Fijian people for the most part have more curly hair then the Indians and that, for the most part, the native Fijians are a stockier, bigger people than the Indians and that the Fijians have broader faces than the Indians, for the most part. There are Indians that look like Fijians and Fijians that look like Indians. It’s really hard to tell walking down the street but the conflict is there and is real.

Working

The fact that I was in Fiji at all is a testament to the Internet. Eight of my students were employees of Vodaphone, a British cell phone company that has the cell phone concession in Fiji and two "students" worked for Datec a training company with an office in Fiji. This was their class. Datec offers consulting and training all over the South Pacific and are listed on the Toronto Stock Exchange.

Vodaphone had asked Datec to create this class for their employees. Datec couldn't find anyone that could teach it so they contacted the Australian division of a company based in Dubai called Flane. They looked on the Internet and found me. When they called I incredulously asked if there really wasn't anyone between Boston Massachusetts USA and Suva Fiji who could teach the class they replied that they couldn't find any. Good news or bad news? I'm either on the cutting edge of the new technology (which is what I like to believe) or I'm just a relic of a passed up branch of technology more suited for academic study than real applications. With competition I'd at least feel validated.

I had 10 people in my class, eight Indians, one Fijian and an "*expat*" Australian. I mention this because it was my first hint of how the Fijian society has segregated and isolated itself. Over the week it became apparent that Indians occupy the professional class in Fiji and if there can be said to be a Middle Class in Fiji they occupy that too.

Seven Days in Fiji

Rotary

I belong to a Rotary club. For those of you who don't know Rotary is an international organization with over 30,000 clubs. Put in its most simple form, Rotary is about world peace and cooperative living. Democrats and Republicans, Conservatives and Liberals, all with capital letters belong to Rotary, its not about politics it's about people organizing to help people. In my town we've paid for part of an industrial fish farm in Guatemala, lit the Christmas trees on the town common, sponsored a literary retreat (wildernesshouse.org) and paid for an industrial therapist to help the town fathers work better together. Our club meets Tuesday mornings for breakfast while most of the other Rotary clubs nearby meet for lunch. This is the pattern all over the world. If you miss one meting you can "makeup" at another club. Our club gets a high "makeup" traffic simply because we are a breakfast club.

In Suva there are four Rotary clubs, three meet for lunch and one meets for dinner. Because I had been imported to teach my class from such a distance I must be important so for the entire week lunch was catered. This is where British gastronomic tastes put a small damper on the beauty of Fiji. I think it can safely be said that British taste in food was vastly superior to the prevailing taste when they first arrived, roasted rump of one's fellow man being rather unappetizing. However there is no excuse for rice and yellow curried chicken followed by rice and chicken with brown curry followed by rice and chicken with black curry and peas. You get the picture. No insult intended but why couldn't I have gotten a job in Tahiti. Since Datec felt they had to cater lunch I felt honor bound to eat it. That prevented me from doing a "makeup" at any of the luncheon Rotary clubs.

I admit that what I am about to say is pure conjecture as I have but the scantiest evidence for it save a list of names. Most towns the size of Suva sport one Rotary club. Suva has four. From the list of members names one is all Fijian, one is all Indian, one is all *expat*, that is, all Aussies and Kiwis and one is a dinner club suitable for making up if you miss the club of your ethnic choice. I managed to do a "makeup" at the Suva Peninsula club, the dinner club.

There were eight of us for dinner at the fanciest Chinese restaurant in Suva. The Rotary club web site said that dinner started at 6:30 so I was there 10 minutes early. I was the first one to show up and began to wonder when no one else had arrived by 6:45. "Fiji time," I was told with a laugh, which means that everything in Fiji starts late. By 7:00 we had 8 Rotarians. I cannot remember most names but on my left was a large Fijian gentleman on the board of some large local corporation. On my right was the President of the club, an *expat*, who ran a canning company. Like all things in Fiji the Fiji Rotary clubs are modeled on their British counterparts. The president wore a ponderous gilded chain around his neck when conducting the meeting. In the states we assume that the man at the podium is the president, an assumption that has yet to fail me.

Of the remaining 5 Rotarians I remember only the two charming women of Indian extraction. The first, Dr. Bernadette, (I was told that I could never pronounce her last name) is a professor of dentistry at the University of the South Pacific as well as President of the Fiji Dental Association. The other was a charming well-healed pharmacist named "Josh," a name that was short for something unpronounceable. Both were charming, animated, and very British and both invited me to be their guests at a meeting of the Fiji-British Alumni Association.

The Fiji-British Alumni Association had been created as an all-inclusive organization where Fijian, Indian and other Commonwealth types could meet and interact. It is the perfect type of an organization for a Rotarian to belong to. Unfortunately the coup d'état of 2000 purged the government of most Indians and put an end to an ecumenical government. The Fiji-British Alumni Association had gone into suspension soon after the coup as ecumenism was frowned on. Time cures most things so the Fiji-British Alumni Association was trying to revive itself. This was its second meeting post coup.

Fortunately the meeting of the Fiji-British Alumni Association was being held at the Fiji Lawn Tennis Association, right down the street from me at the edge of Albert Park, and next to the Cricket game that was still going on. The meeting of the Fiji-British Alumni Association was a completely informal dinner. I wore a jacket and tie, which I quickly shed. The Fiji-British Alumni Association was made up of almost equal parts Fijian and Indian with a reasonable representation of Ausies, New Zealanders and me. After an initial pleasant mix of pleasantries everyone segregated themselves into Fiji and Indian tables. I sat with Dr. Bernadette and Josh.

Apparently, the meeting of the Fiji-British Alumni Association was a major social event with the Fiji Times sending both a reporter and a photographer. Yes my picture was snapped with Dr. Bernadette and Josh but I don't think I made the social column. There was an Indian woman who is a famous Judge, a very big deal I was told. She mugged for the camera and made sure her picture was taken with everyone present. She looked like an old fashioned politician running for office. I mentioned this to Josh who reminded me quietly what the last coup was all about. Apparently there is an *expat* woman that might indeed become a compromise candidate for Prime Minister. Fijian politics is a very strange beast.

I can only hope that Fijians and Indians come to some understanding before someone resorts to violence again. Fiji is a beautiful place with a thin veneer of civilization provided by British institutions but with an unfortunate history of ethnic problems and an equally unfortunate British taste in food. Note to the second edition: Fiji had yet another coup on December 5th 2006.

When the event ended I walked with Dr. Bernadette and Josh to the cabstand on Victoria Parade. We walked pass a group of Fijian youths hanging out with smoke wafting up from their midst. I was enjoying the night and oblivious to the real world around me. “Lets hurry,” Dr. Bernadette whispered to me, “They are smoking marijuana and two Indian girls and middle aged white man are a very good target for mugging.” I didn’t recognize the smell, I grew up in the 1960’s and 70’s, and I still didn’t feel threatened but my escorts did so we hurried.

“It’s a weed,” she said. “Did you know it grows wild here,” Dr. Bernadette asked?

“I think it grows wild almost everywhere it’s allowed,” I answered.

“They found a fully grown pot plant in the courtyard of the Town Counsel building in downtown Suva last summer.” She went on. “You can imagine the furor over that,” she went on with a giggle.

We walked on in silence, giggling to ourselves.

Missions des Pères Maristes en Océanie.
Cueillette du fruit de l'arbre à pain.
Archipel des Fidji.

Monday through Friday

With the exception of my Thursday evening feast at the Fiji-British Alumni Association my week was as predictable as it would have been if my class were in Peoria Illinois. I got up early, had breakfast at the bar/restaurant, taught my class and toured the town looking for a good place to eat and be entertained.

I'm from New England in the northeast corner of the Unite States of America. We have a delicacy found nowhere else on earth, Maple Syrup. We take it for granted and use it (or maple flavored corn syrup if we want to be cheep) liberally on pancakes and waffles for breakfast. To someone used to the maple flavor anything else is … unnatural. Fiji's major export is cane sugar and the syrup of choice is a mild molasses. Breakfast for me became a source of nourishment rather than a celebration of the senses.

In the evenings I scavenged the town like a feral cat in search of a meal. I sniffed at the door of almost every restaurant in town. The choices were between Indian and Chinese cuisine. In most cases I opted for a Chinese appetizer (yes you can ruin a spring roll). Almost every restaurant, both Chinese and Indian, also served "Fish & Chips" which became my staple dinner simply for its lack of curry. On my way home each night I passed the American Embassy where the guards began to recognize me and say hello. I passed the girls and "puftas" assembling for the night's work. After the first night they too said hello and "Have a good night Sir, we're here if you want us." I think it became a sport for them to spot me and say hello. As the week wore on it became a rising chorus. If I had worn a hat I would have tipped it to them. Although I was told that it was a bad corner to pass through I never once felt threatened, the livelihood of to many people depended on the corner being safe and so it was.

One truly remarkable feature of Suva Fiji is the complete lack of Japanese tourists. I'm not sure why but I can speculate that they haven't discovered it yet or there is a lasting distaste for visiting lands once threatened by the rising sun. Should the Japanese ever discover Fiji they will not only improve the cuisine on the islands but also discover that the Fijians also drive on the British side of the street a feature shared only among British Commonwealth countries and Japan. It should be a natural.

There is an active nightlife in Suva but since my body took its time adjusting seven hours to Fiji time I faded well before any of the hot spots got cooking. In Fiji the nightlife begins at 10:00 P.M. and continues well past the legal limit of Midnight. The music on the radios and in the nightclubs is the same in Fiji as it is anywhere in the US. The only difference is that on Radio Fiji the DJ's speak with that ever so delightful British accent.

I had been scheduled to leave Fiji on Saturday as I had come in, a flight from Suva to Nadi and then home. I had mentioned to the manager at Datec that I'd rather take a buss from Suva to Nadi so that I could see the countryside. Would I rather take a cab I was asked. That option never dawned on me since

Suva and Nadi are 200 km apart by car. Of course I'd rather go by car with a knowledgeable guide.

The Ride to Nadi

It was all arranged before I left the Hotel on Friday morning. I would be taking a cab back to Nadi and spend Friday night at the Capricorn Hotel before flying back home. Apparently there is constant cab traffic between Nadi and Suva and if you know the right people you can get a deadheading cab for next to nothing. In my case it was $70 in Fiji dollars, about $40 US for a five-hour ride.

My class was scheduled to be over at 5:00 P.M. and the cab was called for 6. There are lots and lots of cabs in Suva and most of them are pretty run down. You can go from one side of Suva to the other for $1.60 Fiji, about $1.00 US. I was expecting a beat up clunker of a car for the ride to Nadi. I had 24 hours to get to the Nadi airport and if the car broke down (as I was warned that the busses often do) I could still make it one way or the other. I'm adventuress and nothing in Fiji ever instilled any kind of fear in me. When the car arrived, instead of a beat up clunker there was what looked like a brand new Toyota Corolla station wagon. It wasn't a Corolla but rather an underpowered right hand drive car I suspect Toyota makes for the third world market. The maximum speed limit in Fiji is 80 km/hr, about 50 miles per hour. Cars and trucks don't have to be able to achieve the speeds common in the US so all the cars and trucks are underpowered. The Fijians would laugh at us if they knew what kind of mileage we get.

My driver was named Aruind. His cab was decked out in what I have to describe as a combination "American Tuner" and "Indian modern." Occupying the first foot of the back of the station wagon were a set of homebuilt gigantic speakers, the kind that make the ground shake as the car drives by, all base and no treble. On the dashboard was a tasseled red velvet throw that looked to have been tailor made to fit. Hanging from the oversized add-on mirror were more tassels and on the instrument panel was a cutout picture of some unrecognizable Indian god. "You should have ended your class at 4:00 PM," Aruind said in his Indio-British accent, "You will miss the most beautiful sunset anywhere in Fiji."

As we drove out of town I leaned out of the car window to take pictures of "typical" Fijian houses. The typical house, at least on the road between Suva and Nadi, is a single floor wooden structure built on stilts about two feet high with corrugated steel for the roof and both interior and exterior walls. This is common even way up on the hills of Suva. I imagine that his improves air circulation and in low-lying areas helps prevent flooding. There is no need for insulation just protection from wind and rain. There was a time when only Indians lived in these tin sheds but the practically and durability of these structures over the wood and thatch construction of the more typical Fijian house has lead to their adoption by the more urban Fijian population.

A mile or so out of town Aruind turned and asked, “Do you smoke?”

“No,” I answered, “I used to but quit, go ahead if you like.”

Aruind then asked, “You’re an American, right? You know Jamaica?”

“Yes,” I answered cautiously. I wasn’t sure where this was going.

“I can tell from your eyes you know what I’m talking about,” he continued, “Mind if I smoke a spliff?”

“Go ahead,” I answered.

From there the ride got more interesting as Aruind became more animated.

The national speed limit in Fiji is 80 km/hr or about 50 miles per hour and most cars and trucks can only speed on a downhill slope. Aruind wasn't the only cab heading back to Nadi and we played leapfrog with his friends for nearly an hour before loosing them in the dark. At one point we ran into a police checkpoint. We stopped while the police looked all over the vehicle and checked Aruind's drivers license. It was a completely perfunctory roadblock. Aruind and the policemen kept up a banal chatter about sports, the weather and who knows what else while they went through their ritual. After we were waived through, Aruind explained, "No one in Fiji has much respect for the Police so they have to show themselves to the public every once in a while." "Are you impressed now," he asked with a wink as he pulled out another joint.

"I hear it grows wild here in Fiji," I said.

"Nah, maybe in the mountains but drive up any road here and you will find it in everyone's back yard," Aruind said.

I sat back, enjoying the darkening view and the air rushing past my face. Everyone drives with the windows open even at 50 miles per hour. It's too hot to drive with the windows up and to cool to turn on the air-conditioner if you have one. I was slowly falling into that mesmerized state we fall into when presented with endless scenery. When my children were young and restless I could easily put them to sleep by getting in the car and going for a "mystery trip." This was becoming my mystery trip. Aruind suddenly swerved off the road and stopped.

Mystery Trip

"If your class had ended at 4 PM instead of 6 PM," he said, " you would now be looking at the most beautiful sunset in all Fiji. I tried to take a picture of it but it was really to dark. A Google search reveals what I should have seen:

As we drove on into the night we would occasionally drive through Fijian villages. A large sign and a speed bump would precede the village entrance. The speed limit would drop from 80 km/hr to 20 km/hr. Fijian villages at night are a busy place. People milling back and forth with the occasional roadside stand selling roast goat from a charcoal stoked fire. Every house had a front porch with a single fluorescent light welcoming the milling crowd. Every few houses there would be a gathering, men mostly, sitting on the floor drinking *kava* and speaking in hushed tones of the important things while women and children milled about chatting and giggling. Fijians walking along and across the highway as though there was no traffic would occasionally turn, wave a welcome and cry "Bula," welcome. Aruind pushed on. There were long stretches of empty highway and Aruind would gun the engine as we went up and down the hills.

I asked Aruind if there were any large animals that could jump out in front of a car and cause damage? He looked at me quizzically. I told him of the majestic beauty of the American Deer, that prancing, horned animal that grace the forests of Americas Northeast, an animal that will occasionally impale itself on the front of a passing automobile causing catastrophic damage.

Aruind thought for a moment and said with a smile, "There are wild pigs that can run into the street but they don't often cause damage. The only big animals we have here that won't get out of the street and can damage your car are the Fiji people." As we drove along I began to notice that indeed there were lots of "Fiji people" walking along the highway at night along these seemingly lonely stretches of highway.

Fiji is blessed with natural resources in the form an abundance of hydroelectric power. Every shack in Fiji has power but few homes have a landline telephone. Fortunately the cell phone infrastructure is excellent and everyone has a cell phone. We had been driving for almost four hours when Aruind got a cell phone call from his wife. The instructions were to pick up some cousin bring him home and have some tea. Aruind asked if I would I mind a ten-minute detour? Heck no, more adventure.

We turned off the main road and into what looked like a typical suburban subdivision. Aruind's cousin was waiting for us at the intersection and hopped in the back seat. "One town," Aruind said. "Fiji people here, Indian people there," he said as we turned down a small dirt road. We made several turns and finally arrived in Aruind's compound. It was dark out so I may not have seen what was really there but the compound looked like it was perhaps 90 feet long by forty feet wide and enclosed by a six to eight foot tall privet hedge or an equally tall chain link fence covered in vines. We pulled up to an open-ended garage and stopped. For the moment the headlights served as our only light.

Aruind's house had been built by his father and grandfather just a short 100 feet from the Pacific Ocean. Tea was served in the garage. I sat on a bench made from a half log and Aruind sat on a small stool. As we sat sipping tea we talked about the construction. The floor was a poured concrete slab into which 2x4's had been set. Also sets in the concrete were large eyebolts. The walls, both interior and exterior as well as the roof were of corrugated steel. Through each corrugated steel panel ran a quarter inch cable terminating in a turnbuckle at the eyebolts. At the center of each room was a single incandescent light bulb. Enough to see but not enough to do detailed work like reading.

I asked Aruind about cyclones, as hurricanes in this part of the pacific are called. He pulled on a cable and said with a smile, "This house may be underwater in a cyclone but its not going anywhere." Occasionally they get very bad cyclones but Fiji is located directly in the middle of the spawning ground for south pacific Typhoons and as such they are usually relatively mild as they pass by. Fiji had not had a cyclone for five years and Aruind predicted that the next one would be very bad. A lot of building has taken place since then.

Figure 6 Indian settlers in Fiji

Nadi

We continued on to Nadi and my room at the Capricorn Hotel. Aruind had offered me his spare bedroom and I wish I had taken it but I wanted to see Nadi the next morning. We parted with a promise that I'd call him in the morning and that we would tour more of this part of Fiji.

Nadi is on the western part of the island along with the nice weather, the tourist resorts and the Internal airport. If Suva is cheap, Nadi is expensive. Anywhere in Suva costs $1.60 for a cab ride but in Nadi the minimum is $5.00. Nadi itself is not a destination. It's a small town compared with Suva. If you are a rich tourist then you head by boat, airplane, helicopter, seaplane or cab to the resort of your choice. Nicole Kidman was said to be in Fiji when I was there but in a totally different milieu. I am sure that wherever she stayed the food was excellent and the creature comforts identical to those of New York City, London or Paris.

I took the $5.00 (Fiji) cab to Nadi center from my hotel, passed the second McDonalds in Fiji, and walked the length of the town. Nadi is not a very big town and end-to-end is about a ten-minute walk. Since tourists pass through Nadi the pressure to sell and sell quickly is far greater in Nadi than in Suva. I walked down the main street and allowed myself to be drawn into a store selling reproductions of Fijian battle instruments and carved toys. My intension was to buy a $20 souvenir. I am pretty good about sticking to my intensions so I was not afraid of a full sales broadside. I always assume that I might learn something from these exchanges.

My "personal" salesman introduced himself as Steve. Fijians adopt English names but often pronounce them differently enough to become unrecognizable. In this case my salesman spoke perfect British English and knew enough Americanisms to be almost annoying. I want local authenticity not an imitation of where I'm escaping from. Nadi is full of these Americanisms. There is a pizza restaurant run by an *expat* Australian woman.

There is a McDonald's and then there is the "Texas" clothing store, which sells blue jeans and other western gear, made in Indonesia.

The store I was in was named "Bula," which means something like *welcome* or *ciao* or just *hello*. Everyone says *bula*, even people on the street whose eyes you catch by accident. Every other store in Fiji has "bula" as part of its name.

This particular store sold handicrafts and I was determined to buy a trinket. In most stores around the world you explore the merchandise, with or without the help of a store clerk or personal salesman and I began to explore the shop on my own. Steve, my personal salesman, said, "No before we shop we must have *kava*." He asked me if I had ever had kava and indeed I never had. Kava is one of those drinks that make you wonder if there is a hidden drug in it. I was suspicious but willing to suspend judgment.

The ceremony begins with everyone sitting cross-legged on the floor. The kava powder is mixed in a large wooden bowl with some kind of ornament pointed at the guest of honor. Since I had the credit cards I was the guest of honor. Kava is a made from the root of a plant closely related to the black pepper plant. According to the Wikipedia:

> **Kavalactones** are the main psychoactive components of the roots of kava[vii], a shrub. … The rhizome and roots of the shrub are ground, grated and steeped in water to produce a non-alcoholic drink which is said to promote sociability, mental clarity, and

> reduction of anxiety*)*. The quantity and ratio of kavalactones present vary dramatically and are highest when roots are extracted with solvents rather than by conventional tea. … Effects of kavalactones include mild sedation, a slight numbing of the gums and mouth, and vivid dreams. Kava has been reported to improve cognitive performance and promote a cheerful mood. Muscle relaxant, anaesthetic, anticonvulsive and anxiolytic effects are thought to result from direct interactions of kavalactones with voltage-dependent ion channels

Yikes! What was I about to drink? After mixing the powder with water, stirring it for a minute or so the master of ceremony handed me a small half coconut shell filled with a white milky fluid. I was told I had to chug the drink after everyone clapped three times. So clap, clap, clap, and I emptied the coconut bowl. Kava tastes roughly like watered down un-flavored Kaopectate, that chalk filled drink that stops diarrhea. We clapped three times and everyone chugged a cup of kava until the bowel was emptied. Besides the slight numbing of my lips Kava was not a memorable experience.

Steve then proceeded to try to sell me everything in the store. I ended up buying a small, carved sea turtle for $50 that I should have paid about $20, the power of kava. I might have done the same if I had been offered an espresso.

Towns are a place where commerce takes place. Even if the primary occupation in a town like Nadi is to sell things and services to tourists there is always a component that services the local population. Off in the back of the town there is a large market. Part of the market is in the open air and part in an enormous shed. The most colorful part of this outdoor market was the spice and vegetable market.

I walked through the market wishing I could buy everything in sight if only for the color feast.

I walked though the market, passed the piles of kava root, pineapples and fish and emerged in a large square surrounded by shops and restaurants. In Boston we have Faneuil Hall[viii]; Nadi has *this* square. I get the same feeling of hurried commerce in both places.

At the far end of the square was “Bula Bargains”, a charming local equivalent of a K-Mart having their pre-Christmas sale. They had small plastic electrically lit Christmas trees, made in India and laughing Santa’s made in China. It’s a world wide economy.

Nadi is a small town and I had seen most of what I wanted to see so I paid $5.00 and went back the Capricorn Hotel and checked out.

I had promised to call Aruind in the morning for some more guided sightseeing. I thought I could call from the hotel but they had a 10 A.M. checkout policy and I was out of the room and all paid up so why should anyone let me use a phone. Public phone, what is a public phone? The Hotel didn't have one … but there was one half a mile down the street. So I went looking and found a public phone. It didn't take coins or standard credit cards, just a TelcomFiji prepaid phone card. I didn't have one and I didn't see any stores nearby that looked like they might have one so I went back to the hotel thinking I might have to take a cab back to Nadi just to call Aruind. Fortunately every hotel catering to tourists has a store that sells everything you need and lots you don't. I bought a "telecard" for $3.00 Fiji and headed back out to call Aruind. Aruind was at the store but he would come get me as soon as he got back, assured his wife. I went back to the hotel and fell asleep by the pool. I'm not sure how long I was asleep but Aruind came over to me and woke me up, with a start. “Lets go,” he almost screamed, “We have things to see.”

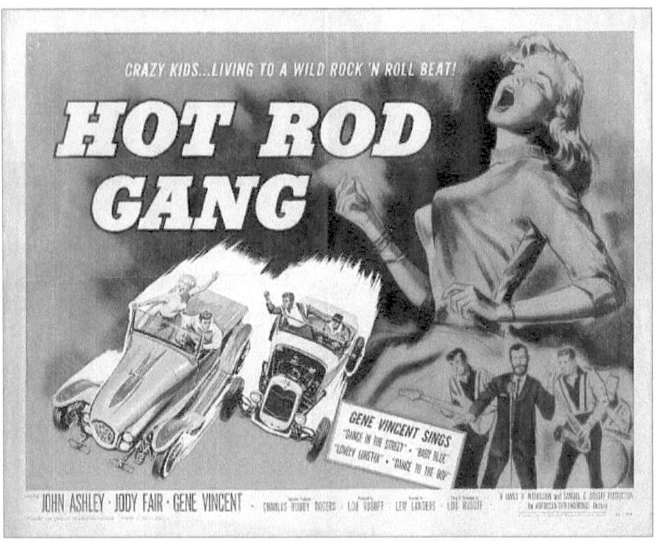

A Fine-Tuned Hot-Rod

I hopped into his station wagon and we were off to the beach. It was not one of the gorgeous beaches you see in the flyers but rather the Nadi town beach. We parked at the end of a dead end street and just talked about everything under the sun with the beach and mountains in the background. Aruind was ambitious. His passion was his car and he lamented the high cost of the accessories that would make his car unique among cabs.

Figure 7 Nadi Town Beach

Back in the 1950's when I was a small kid we used to drive into town on Saturday nights and watch the "greasers," teenagers and older who wore tight black pants, greased slicked back hair and rebuilt cars from the 1930's into Hot-Rods. Hot-Rods were the 1950's expression of America's car culture. Today they are called "tuners" and while the average slightly geeky "tuner" may not relate to the "greaser" of old their passion for rebuilding autos is just as intense.

Hot-Rods would announce their presence by the throaty roar of the straight-through unmuffled pipes. The direct decedents of these hot-rodders are the owners of chopped Harley-Davidson motorcycles whose rumble en mass can be heard from miles away. Today's hot-rodders, tuners, rumble through town in camouflaged Honda, Toyota and Volkswagen sedans. You will only know the car is a tuner when the occupants crank up the volume on their overpowered stereos. Most unmodified cars have amplifiers that power their speakers with as much as 50 or 60 watts. Crank it all the way up and most people will feel 120 decibels of real pain and quickly turn it down.

Figure 8 Aruind at Nadi Town Beach

Aruind is tuner. Tuners turn the entire cavity of their autos into drastically overpowered sub woofers pushing as much as 1000 watts. These are the cars that rumble through the streets, shaking nearby houses with a rhythmic earthquake as they pass by. Tuners, while more sedate than their candy apple red and metallic lime hot-rod ancestors still want to dress up their more or less ordinary looking cars. A Honda Civic with rotating chromed hubcaps is a "way cool" tuner addition. If you added "Mag" hubcaps, fluorescent and metallic fire appliqué and a 1000-watt stereo system to Aruind's Toyota station wagon and you have Aruind's dream cab. Add a red and blue flashing fluorescent tubes under the hood (the red timed to look like bursts of fire as the car revs up) and Aruind, being a Hindu, would think he had died and been reborn in Detroit.

Another Mystery Trip

We drove along the shore road and into the sugar cane area paralleling the narrow gage railroad.

Between Nadi and Lautoka, the town just around the bend from Nadi, are a number of sights worth seeing. The mountains you see when you get off the airplane in Nadi are called "the Sleeping Giants," and they do look like a man and a woman sleeping on their backs. At the base of the "Sleeping Giants" is the Garden of the Sleeping Giant. This famous orchard garden, a combined commercial nursery and fantasy garden, was once owned by actor Raymond Burr (Perry Mason). It was closed on Saturday so I'll have to live with Aruind's description of it, which included every color known to exist in the English language.

Past the entrance to the Sleeping Garden are the Guns of Lomolomo. Fiji is just one stop beyond the last island Japan occupied during WWII and if not for the battle of the Coral Sea Fiji might well have been occupied. The Guns of Lomolomo, one gun actually, is a remnant of the need to protect the Nadi airport from marauding Japanese ships. The guns are actually remounted 6-inch British navel guns with a provenance that includes the Boer War and the relief of Mafeking during WW I. We would have had to climb up a steep hill and over private property to see them and neither Aruind nor I were feeling that energetic so we pressed on to Lautoka, Fiji's second largest city. Lautoka was built on sugarcane and all the narrow gage railways that wind up each of the valleys end at the massive sugar refinery almost at the end of the main dock.

The area where the city of Lautoka now stands was first sighted by Captain Bligh of HMS Bounty who rowed ashore with loyal crewmembers after the famous mutiny. Lautoka is also the landing spot where thousands of indentured Indians first came ashore to work the sugarcane fields and refinery. The sugar harvest had just ended and the yards were full of empty railcars.

Aruind and I sat on the seawall in Lautoka telling stories and speculating on what we could do to make our fortunes. I suggested importing a French Chief, or two, from Tahiti. Aruind gave me a curious look when I said that. Later, when I was at the airport, I ate a slice of pizza at an airport stand. To my surprise it was relatively good. Relative in that it was the best tasting food I had eaten all week. As I was enjoying myself I noticed two young women with backpacks in their early twenties looking very hungry. I knew what they were going through so I mentioned to them that the pizza was actually good. Both gave me a very sour look and one said, "Please, we are going to wait until we are in Los Angeles to eat. We've had the most disgusting food for the last two weeks here in Fiji."

Aruind said that he knew how he could make a fortune. All he needed was a container full of auto parts. I laughed and reminded him that in America I was not a rich man. "OK," he said, "then send me three sets of *mag* hubcaps, one set for my cab so that I can advertise and two to sell. We'll split the profits; we'll make a fortune."

I don’t know cars but I intend to send Aruind whatever I can find. If you would like to go into the auto-parts business with a hustling Indian entrepreneur in Fiji Aruind can be found at:

Aruind Keshwal
PO Box 9368
Nadi Airport
Fiji Islands

His phone number is 9951187

Figure 9 Sugarcane refinery in Lautoka

One More Stop

It was getting late and Aruind said we had to make one more stop. He wanted me to meet his sister and his "auntie." We drove back in the direction of Nadi but turned up a dirt road and, after making several turns ended up in front of another corrugated steel house nestled in the middle of a small compound of similar houses. Indians tend to have more furniture than Fijians and Aruind's sisters house was no exception. On the right as you walk in was a large couch and an overstuffed chair. On the left was a dining room table while overhead the standard bare light bulb. All about the room on various pieces of furniture were small shrines including one apparently dedicated to a Snoopy who occupied the central position in a shrine surrounded by candles and cloth. Aruind's sister and "auntie" were interested in how I celebrated Christmas while I was interested in their daily lives. When I described putting colored balls and lights on a pine tree Aruind's sister pointed to a small, decorated plastic tree in the corner of the room. In her pantheon a Christmas tree deserves its own shrine.

When we got around to her life and situation I was a bit circumspect. Most places I've been to partially define "middleclass" as a household where the women don't work outside the home. By this definition most of America has fallen back into the role of working class without admitting it. If I asked Aruind's sister what she did for work I thought I might insult her but that is exactly what I wanted to know. Aruind understood why I was being timid and said, "Fiji has no middle class, all rich and poor, nothing in the middle." That took care of my reluctance to ask Aruind's sister how she spent her days.

If I were in China or some other country known to be politically dangerous I might have been a bit more attuned when listening to her nuanced answers. At the time her pleasant and matter of fact delivery lulled me into mentally just recording the facts about jobs in Fiji. It is only now, some weeks removed from the events that allow me to understand exactly what is happening in Fiji. A while back I recorded my impression of the history of Fiji. My history more or less ended about the time Fiji gained independence from Britain. Let me bring you up to date.

Fiji is a multicultural society living under the thin veneer of British Civilization. I put that in capital letters to emphasize what everyone in Fiji truly believes in their more sane moments. Fiji is, for all intents, 50% Fijian and 50% Indian. In the 1990's Fiji created a constitution that was truly multicultural. The first president of Fiji with Indian blood in his veins was elected and it was beginning to look like Fiji had made or was poised to make a leap few countries ever make to a racially mixed, racially blind democracy. It was not to be. The Fijian party controls the police and the army and most of the land in Fiji is controlled and communally owned by Fijians leaving Indians as permanent second-class citizens. The coup of 2000 effectively removed all Indians from the government and sent packing hundreds of Indian businessmen with investments on the islands. The Fijian counsel of Chiefs, that holdover from pre-Colonial days now appoints the President who may or may not accept the Prime Minister elected by parliament. Democracy is a fragile form of government, there will always be people who don't like the outcome of popular expression and will seek to pervert its institutions.

Aruind's sister had been employed in a textile factory that closed soon after the coup and has not reopened. Working in the textile factory was almost the only hope of attaining a middle class income and life style in Fiji. We, in America, may scoff at textile workers earning a small fraction of what we do but to them it is a lot of money. Just $2.00 US an hour would bring an income more than the national average in Fiji.

Time was running out but before I could go I had to have more kava. Aruind explained that beer and wine were too expensive for the average Fijian so kava was the national drink for everyone, Indian and Fijian alive. We all clapped and I was handed the small coconut filled with the dusty liquid, which I chugged. Aruind made his kava considerably stronger than the kava I had had in Nadi. My lips were immediately numbed. "What is this supposed to do," I asked? Aruind laughed and said, "It's very good for family planning. It numbs everything"

I needed to use the facilities, which gave me the opportunity to explore the house. I've already described the "living room." The bedrooms were unadorned mattresses on the wooden floor with a small bureau. The kitchen was in an adjacent corrugated steel covered porch with a hibachi. The facilities I was seeking were behind the house in a separate row of "outhouses" with flush toilets. A small Indian neighbor girl, giggling with curiosity waved at me from her back yard.

It was dark as we left the house. On the way to the airport I asked Aruind how well he could read if I sent him a letter. “Dear boy,” he said, “I passed the fifth form.” That’s 11th grade I thought, I’ll have to send him a postcard … and some auto parts.

The airplane ride home was uneventful. If there was turbulence I slept soundly through it. I had left Nadi airport at 10:30 P.M. on a Saturday evening. I arrived at 6:00 A.M Monday morning in Boston. I have a seven-hour jet lag or is it 17 hours and it snowed 10 inches last night.

Figure 10 Steve Glines is a writer with a sunburn from Fiji

Footnotes

[i] http://www.fiji.pictures-pacific.com/viti-levu/index.html
[ii] http://en.wikipedia.org/wiki/20th_Century_Limited

The 20th Century Limited was an express passenger train operated by the New York Central Railroad from 1902 to 1967, during which time it would become known as a "National Institution" and the "Most Famous Train in the World." In the year of its last run, The New York Times said that it "...was known to railroad buffs for 65 years as the world's greatest train." The train traveled between Grand Central Terminal in New York City and LaSalle Street Station in Chicago, Illinois along the railroad's famed "Water Level Route". The NYC inaugurated this train as direct competition to the Pennsylvania Railroad's Broadway Limited, both lines intended for upper class as well as business travelers between the two cities. Making few station stops along the way and as few breaks for water and coal as possible, trains on this route routinely could make the 800-mile (1300 km) journey in only fifteen and one-half hours (roughly 50 mph or 85 km/h).

Known for its speed as well as for its style, passengers walked to and from the train on a plush, crimson carpet which was rolled out at station stops and specially designed for the 20th Century Limited. Thus, the "red carpet treatment" was born. The locomotive and passenger cars were designed in an Art Deco style in blues and grays (the colors of the New York Central).

By the late 1950s the train was in decline. On December 2, 1967 at 6 p.m. the train left Grand Central Terminal on track 34 for the last time, half full. As always, carnations were given to men boarding the train, and perfume and flowers to the women. The next day, it straggled into LaSalle Street Station in Chicago nine hours late.

Today, Amtrak operates a route called the Lake Shore Limited, which travels almost exactly along the same path as the 20th Century. The only differences are at the two ends - at the New York end it runs to Penn Station, and on the Chicago end it switches to the former Pennsylvania Railroad's

---

Pittsburgh, Fort Wayne and Chicago Railway at Whiting, Indiana, running into Union Station.

[iii] http://www.harryflashman.org/

[iv] http://acc6.its.brooklyn.cuny.edu/~phalsall/texts/chinhist.html

THE REPUBLIC OF CHINA (1912-1949)

Early in March 1912, Sun Yat-sen resigned from the presidency and, as promised, Yuan Shih-kai was elected his successor at Nanjing. Inaugurated in March 1912 in Beijing, the base of his power, Yuan established a republican system of government with a premier, a cabinet, a draft constitution, and a plan for parliamentary elections early in 1913. The Kuomintang (KMT, National People's party), the successor to Sun Yat-sen's organization, was formed in order to prepare for the election.

Despite his earlier pledges to support the republic, Yuan schemed to assassinate his opponents and weaken the constitution and the parliament. By the end of 1914 he had made himself president for life and even planned to establish an imperial dynasty with himself as the first emperor. His dream was thwarted by the serious crisis of the Twenty-one Demands for special privileges presented by the Japanese in January 1915 and by vociferous opposition from many sectors of Chinese society. He died in June 1916 a broken man. After Yuan's death, a number of his proteges took positions of power in the Beijing government or ruled as warlords in outlying regions. In August 1917 the Beijing government joined the Allies and declared war on Germany. At the peace conference in Versailles, France, the Chinese demand to end foreign concessions in China was ignored.

Sun-yat Sen (1866-1925). Known as the father of modern China, Sun Yat-sen worked to achieve his lofty goals for modern China. These included the overthrow of the Manchu Dynasty, the unification of China, and the establishment of a republic.

Sun Yat-sen was born on Nov. 12, 1866, in Guangdong Province and attended several schools, including one in Honolulu, Hawaii, before transferring to a college of medicine in Hong Kong. Graduating in 1892, Sun almost immediately abandoned medicine for politics. His role in an unsuccessful uprising in Canton in 1895 prompted Sun to begin an exile that lasted for 16 years. Sun used this time to travel widely in Japan, Europe, and the United States, enlisting sympathy and raising money for his republican cause. Sun returned to China in 1911 after a successful rebellion in Wuhan inspired uprisings in other provinces. As leader of the Kuomintang, or Nationalist party, Sun was elected provisional president of the newly declared republic but was forced to resign in 1912.

In 1913 his disagreements with government policies led Sun to organize a second revolution. Failing to regain power, Sun left once again for Japan, where he organized a separate government. Sun returned to China and attempted to set up a new government in 1917 and 1921 before successfully installing himself as generalissimo of a new regime in 1923.

Sun increasingly relied on aid from the Soviet Union, and in 1924 he reorganized the Kuomintang on the model of the Soviet Communist party. Sun also founded the Whampoa Military Academy and appointed Chiang Kai-shek as its president. Sun summarized his policies in the Three Principles of the People--nationalism, democracy, and socialism. He died of cancer in Peking on March 12, 1925. Sun's tomb in Nanking is now a national shrine.

The May Fourth Movement.

After World War I The Chinese felt betrayed. Anger and frustration erupted in demonstrations on May 4, 1919, in Beijing. Joined by workers and merchants, the movement spread to major cities. The Chinese representative at Versailles refused to endorse the peace treaty, but its provisions remained unchanged. Disillusioned with the West, many Chinese looked elsewhere for help.

The May Fourth Movement, which grew out of the student uprising, attacked Confucianism, initiated a vernacular style of writing, and promoted science. Scholars of international stature, such as John Dewey and Bertrand Russell, were invited to lecture. Numerous magazines were published to stimulate new thoughts. Toward the end of the movement's existence, a split occurred among its leaders. Some, like Ch'en Tu-hsiu and Li Ta-chao, were beginning to be influenced by the success of the Russian Revolution of 1917, which contrasted sharply with the failure of the 1911 Revolution in China to change the social order and improve conditions. By 1920, people associated with the Comintern (Communist International) were disseminating literature in China and helping to start Communist groups, including one led by Mao Zedong. A meeting at Shanghai in 1921 was actually the first party congress of the Communist Party of China (CCP).

The CCP was so small that the Soviet Union looked elsewhere for a viable political ally. A Comintern agent, Adolph Joffe, was sent to China to approach Sun Yat-sen, who had failed to obtain assistance from Great Britain or the United States. The period of Sino-Soviet collaboration began with the Sun-Joffe Declaration of Jan. 26, 1923. The KMT was recognized by the Soviet Union, and the Communists were admitted as members. With Soviet aid, the KMT army was built up. A young officer, Chiang Kai-shek, was sent to Moscow for training. Upon returning, he was put in charge of the Whampoa Military Academy, established to train soldiers to fight the warlords, who controlled much of China S(See Chiang Kai-shek). Zhou Enlai (also Chou En-lai) of the CCP was deputy director of the academy's political department.

Sun Yat-sen, whose power base was in the south, had planned to send an expedition against the northern warlords, but he died before it could get under way. Chiang Kai-shek, who succeeded him in the KMT leadership, began the northern expedition in July 1926. The Nationalist army met little resistance and by April 1927 had reached the lower Yangtze. Meanwhile, Chiang, claiming to be a sincere follower of Sun Yat-sen, had broken with the left-wing elements of the KMT. After the Nationalist forces had taken Shanghai, a Communist-led general strike was suppressed with bloodshed. Following suppressions in other cities, Chiang set up his own government at Nanjing on April 18, 1927. He professed friendship with the Soviet Union, but by July 1927 he was expelling Communists from the KMT. Some left-wingers left for the Soviet Union.

The northern expedition was resumed, and in 1928 Chiang took Peking. China was formally unified. Nationalist China was recognized by the Western powers and supported by loans from foreign banks.

[v] http://tinyurl.com/99hdr or http://www.cbsnews.com/stories/2005/12/13/world/main1119918.shtml

[vi] http://www.literature.org/authors/london-jack/south-sea-tales/chapter-02.html

Chapter 2 - The Whale Tooth

It was in the early days in Fiji, when John Starhurst arose in the mission house at Rewa Village and announced his intention of carrying the gospel throughout all Viti Levu. Now Viti Levu means the "Great Land," it being the largest island in a group composed of many large islands, to say nothing of hundreds of small ones. Here and there on the coasts, living by most precarious tenure, was a sprinkling of missionaries, traders, b^che-de-mer fishers, and whaleship deserters. The smoke of the hot ovens arose under their windows, and the bodies of the slain were dragged by their doors on the way to the feasting.

The Lotu, or the Worship, was progressing slowly, and, often, in crablike fashion. Chiefs, who announced themselves Christians and were welcomed into the body of the chapel, had a distressing habit of backsliding in order to partake of the flesh of some favorite enemy. Eat or be eaten had been the law of the land; and eat or be eaten promised to remain the law of the land for a long time to come. There were chiefs, such as Tanoa, Tuiveikoso, and Tuikilakila, who had literally eaten hundreds of their fellow men. But among these gluttons Ra Undreundre ranked highest. Ra Undreundre lived at Takiraki.

He kept a register of his gustatory exploits. A row of stones outside his house marked the bodies he had eaten. This row was two hundred and thirty paces long, and the stones in it numbered eight hundred and seventy-two. Each stone represented a body. The row of stones might have been longer, had not Ra Undreundre unfortunately received a spear in the small of his back in a bush skirmish on Somo Somo and been served up on the table of Naungavuli, whose mediocre string of stones numbered only forty-eight.

The hard-worked, fever-stricken missionaries stuck doggedly to their task, at times despairing, and looking forward for some special manifestation, some outburst of Pentecostal fire that would bring a glorious harvest of souls. But cannibal Fiji had remained obdurate. The frizzle-headed man-eaters were loath to leave their fleshpots so long as the harvest of human carcases was plentiful. Sometimes, when the harvest was too plentiful, they imposed on the missionaries by letting the word slip out that on such a day there would be a killing and a barbecue. Promptly the missionaries would buy the lives of the victims with stick tobacco, fathoms of calico, and quarts of trade beads. Natheless the chiefs drove a handsome trade in thus disposing of their surplus live meat. Also, they could always go out and catch more.

It was at this juncture that John Starhurst proclaimed that he would carry the Gospel from coast to coast of the Great Land, and that he would begin by penetrating the mountain fastnesses of the headwaters of the Rewa River. His words were received with consternation.

The native teachers wept softly. His two fellow missionaries strove to dissuade him. The King of Rewa warned him that the mountain dwellers would surely kai-kai him--kai-kai meaning "to eat"--and that he, the King of Rewa, having become Lotu, would be put to the necessity of going to war with the mountain dwellers. That he could not conquer them he was perfectly aware. That they might come down the river and sack Rewa Village he was likewise perfectly aware. But what was he to do? If John Starhurst persisted in going out and being eaten, there would be a war that would cost hundreds of lives.

Later in the day a deputation of Rewa chiefs waited upon John Starhurst. He heard them patiently, and argued patiently with them, though he abated not a whit from his purpose. To his fellow missionaries he explained that he was not bent upon martyrdom; that the call had come for him to carry the Gospel into Viti Levu, and that he was merely obeying the Lord's wish.

To the traders who came and objected most strenuously of all, he said: "Your objections are valueless. They consist merely of the damage that may be done your businesses. You are interested in making money, but I am interested in saving souls. The heathen of this dark land must be saved."

John Starhurst was not a fanatic. He would have been the first man to deny the imputation. He was eminently sane and practical.

He was sure that his mission would result in good, and he had private visions of igniting the Pentecostal spark in the souls of the mountaineers and of inaugurating a revival that would sweep down out of the mountains and across the length and breadth of the Great Land from sea to sea and to the isles in the midst of the sea. There were no wild lights in his mild gray eyes, but only calm resolution and an unfaltering trust in the Higher Power that was guiding him.

One man only he found who approved of his project, and that was Ra Vatu, who secretly encouraged him and offered to lend him guides to the first foothills. John Starhurst, in turn, was greatly pleased by Ra Vatu's conduct. From an incorrigible heathen, with a heart as black as his practices, Ra Vatu was beginning to emanate light. He even spoke of becoming Lotu. True, three years before he had expressed a similar intention, and would have entered the church had not John Starhurst entered objection to his bringing his four wives along with him. Ra Vatu had had economic and ethical objections to monogamy. Besides, the missionary's hair-splitting objection had offended him; and, to prove that he was a free agent and a man of honor, he had swung his huge war club over Starhurst's head. Starhurst had escaped by rushing in under the club and holding on to him until help arrived. But all that was now forgiven and forgotten. Ra Vatu was coming into the church, not merely as a converted heathen, but as a converted polygamist as well. He was only waiting, he assured Starhurst, until his oldest wife, who was very sick, should die.

John Starhurst journeyed up the sluggish Rewa in one of Ra Vatu's canoes. This canoe was to carry him for two days, when, the head of navigation reached, it would return. Far in the distance, lifted into the sky, could be seen the great smoky mountains that marked the backbone of the Great Land. All day John Starhurst gazed at them with eager yearning.

Sometimes he prayed silently. At other times he was joined in prayer by Narau, a native teacher, who for seven years had been Lotu, ever since the day he had been saved from the hot oven by Dr. James Ellery Brown at the trifling expense of one hundred sticks of tobacco, two cotton blankets, and a large bottle of painkiller. At the last moment, after twenty hours of solitary supplication and prayer, Narau's ears had heard the call to go forth with John Starhurst on the mission to the mountains.

"Master, I will surely go with thee," he had announced.

John Starhurst had hailed him with sober delight. Truly, the Lord was with him thus to spur on so broken-spirited a creature as Narau.

"I am indeed without spirit, the weakest of the Lord's vessels," Narau explained, the first day in the canoe.

"You should have faith, stronger faith," the missionary chided him.

Another canoe journeyed up the Rewa that day. But it journeyed an hour astern, and it took care not to be seen. This canoe was also the property of Ra Vatu. In it was Erirola, Ra Vatu's first cousin and trusted henchman; and in the small basket that never left his hand was a whale tooth. It was a magnificent tooth, fully six inches long, beautifully proportioned, the ivory turned yellow and purple with age. This tooth was likewise the property of Ra Vatu; and in Fiji, when such a tooth goes forth, things usually happen. For this is the virtue of the whale tooth: Whoever accepts it cannot refuse the request that may accompany it or follow it. The request may be anything from a human life to a tribal alliance, and no Fijian is so dead to honor as to deny the request when once the tooth has been accepted. Sometimes the request hangs fire, or the fulfilment is delayed, with untoward consequences.

High up the Rewa, at the village of a chief, Mongondro by name, John Starhurst rested at the end of the second day of the journey. In the morning, attended by Narau, he expected to start on foot for the smoky mountains that were now green and velvety with nearness. Mongondro was a sweet-tempered, mild-mannered little old chief, short-sighted and afflicted with elephantiasis, and no longer inclined toward the turbulence of war. He received the missionary with warm hospitality, gave him food from his own table, and even discussed religious matters with him. Mongondro was of an inquiring bent of mind, and pleased John Starhurst greatly by asking him to account for the existence and beginning of things. When the missionary had finished his summary of the Creation according to Genesis, he saw that Mongondro was deeply affected. The little old chief smoked silently for some time. Then he took the pipe from his mouth and shook his head sadly.

"It cannot be," he said. "I, Mongondro, in my youth, was a good workman with the adze. Yet three months did it take me to make a canoe--a small canoe, a very small canoe. And you say that all this land and water was made by one man--"

"Nay, was made by one God, the only true God," the missinary interrupted.

"It is the same thing," Mongondro went on, "that all the land and all the water, the trees, the fish, and bush and mountains, the sun, the moon, and the stars, were made in six days! No, no. I tell you that in my youth I was an able man, yet did it require me three months for one small canoe. It is a story to frighten children with; but no man can believe it."

"I am a man," the missionary said.

"True, you are a man. But it is not given to my dark understanding to know what you believe."

"I tell you, I do believe that everything was made in six days." "So you say, so you say," the old cannibal murmured soothingly.

It was not until after John Starhurst and Narau had gone off to bed that Erirola crept into the chief's house, and, after diplomatic speech, handed the whale tooth to Mongondro.

The old chief held the tooth in his hands for a long time. It was a beautiful tooth, and he yearned for it. Also, he divined the request that must accompany it. "No, no; whale teeth were beautiful," and his mouth watered for it, but he passed it back to Erirola with many apologies.

. . . .

In the early dawn John Starhurst was afoot, striding along the bush trail in his big leather boots, at his heels the faithful Narau, himself at the heels of a naked guide lent him by Mongondro to show the way to the next village, which was reached by midday. Here a new guide showed the way. A mile in the rear plodded Erirola, the whale tooth in the basket slung on his shoulder. For two days more he brought up the missionary's rear, offering the tooth to the village chiefs. But village after village refused the tooth. It followed so quickly the missionary's advent that they divined the request that would be made, and would have none of it.

They were getting deep into the mountains, and Erirola took a secret trail, cut in ahead of the missionary, and reached the stronghold of the Buli of Gatoka. Now the Buli was unaware of John Starhurst's imminent arrival. Also, the tooth was beautiful--an extraordinary specimen, while the coloring of it was of the rarest order. The tooth was presented publicly. The Buli of Gatoka, seated on his best mat, surrounded by his chief men, three busy fly-brushers at his back, deigned to receive from the hand of his herald the whale tooth presented by Ra

Vatu and carried into the mountains by his cousin, Erirola. A clapping of hands went up at the acceptance of the present, the assembled headman, heralds, and fly-brushers crying aloud in chorus:

"A! woi! woi! woi! A! woi! woi! woi! A tabua levu! woi! woi! A mudua, mudua, mudua!'

"Soon will come a man, a white man," Erirola began, after the proper pause. "He is a missionary man, and he will come today. Ra Vatu is pleased to desire his boots. He wishes to present them to his good friend, Mongondro, and it is in his mind to send them with the feet along in them, for Mongondro is an old man and his teeth are not good. Be sure, O Buli, that the feet go along in the boots. As for the rest of him, it may stop here."

The delight in the whale tooth faded out of the Buli's eyes, and he glanced about him dubiously. Yet had he already accepted the tooth.

"A little thing like a missionary does not matter," Erirola prompted.

"No, a little thing like a missionary does not matter," the Buli answered, himself again. "Mongondro shall have the boots. Go, you young men, some three or four of you, and meet the missionary on the trail. Be sure you bring back the boots as well."

"It is too late," said Erirola. "Listen! He comes now."

Breaking through the thicket of brush, John Starhurst, with Narau close on his heels, strode upon the scene. The famous boots, having filled in wading the stream, squirted fine jets of water at every step. Starhurst looked about him with flashing eyes. Upborne by an unwavering trust, untouched by doubt or fear, he exulted in all he saw. He knew that since the beginning of time he was the first white man ever to tread the mountain stronghold of Gatoka.

The grass houses clung to the steep mountain side or overhung the rushing Rewa. On either side towered a mighty precipice. At the best, three hours of sunlight penetrated that narrow gorge. No cocoanuts nor bananas were to be seen, though dense, tropic vegetation overran everything, dripping in airy festoons from the sheer lips of the precipices and running riot in all the crannied ledges. At the far end of the gorge the Rewa leaped eight hundred feet in a single span, while the atmosphere of the rock fortress pulsed to the rhythmic thunder of the fall.

From the Buli's house, John Starhurst saw emerging the Buli and his followers.

"I bring you good tidings," was the missionary's greeting.

"Who has sent you?" the Buli rejoined quietly.

"God."

"It is a new name in Viti Levu," the Buli grinned. "Of what islands, villages, or passes may he be chief?"

"He is the chief over all islands, all villages, all passes," John Starhurst answered solemnly. "He is the Lord over heaven and earth, and I am come to bring His word to you."

"Has he sent whale teeth?" was the insolent query.

"No, but more precious than whale teeth is the--"

"It is the custom, between chiefs, to send whale teeth," the Buli interrupted.

"Your chief is either a niggard, or you are a fool, to come empty-handed into the mountains. Behold, a more generous than you is before you."

So saying, he showed the whale tooth he had received from Erirola.

Narau groaned.

"It is the whale tooth of Ra Vatu," he whispered to Starhurst. "I know it well. Now are we undone."

"A gracious thing," the missionary answered, passing his hand through his long beard and adjusting his glasses. "Ra Vatu has arranged that we should be well received."

But Narau groaned again, and backed away from the heels he had dogged so faithfully.

"Ra Vatu is soon to become Lotu," Starhurst explained, "and I have come bringing the Lotu to you."

"I want none of your Lotu," said the Buli, proudly. "And it is in my mind that you will be clubbed this day."

The Buli nodded to one of his big mountaineers, who stepped forward, swinging a club. Narau bolted into the nearest house, seeking to hide among the woman and mats; but John Starhurst sprang in under the club and threw his arms around his executioner's neck. From this point of vantage he proceeded to argue. He was arguing for his life, and he knew it; but he was neither excited nor afraid.

"It would be an evil thing for you to kill me," he told the man. "I have done you no wrong, nor have I done the Buli wrong."

So well did he cling to the neck of the one man that they dared not strike with their clubs. And he continued to cling and to dispute for his life with those who clamored for his death.

"I am John Starhurst," he went on calmly. "I have labored in Fiji for three years, and I have done it for no profit. I am here among you for good. Why should any man kill me? To kill me will not profit any man."

The Buli stole a look at the whale tooth. He was well paid for the deed.

The missionary was surrounded by a mass of naked savages, all struggling to get at him. The death song, which is the song of the oven, was raised, and his expostulations could no longer be heard. But so cunningly did he twine and wreathe his body about his captor's that the death blow could not be struck. Erirola smiled, and the Buli grew angry.

"Away with you!" he cried. "A nice story to go back to the coast--a dozen of you and one missionary, without weapons, weak as a woman, overcoming all of you."

"Wait, O Buli," John Starhurst called out from the thick of the scuffle, "and I will overcome even you. For my weapons are Truth and Right, and no man can withstand them."

"Come to me, then," the Buli answered, "for my weapon is only a poor miserable club, and, as you say, it cannot withstand you."

The group separated from him, and John Starhurst stood alone, facing the Buli, who was leaning on an enormous, knotted warclub.

"Come to me, missionary man, and overcome me," the Buli challenged.

"Even so will I come to you and overcome you," John Starhurst made answer, first wiping his spectacles and settling them properly, then beginning his advance.

The Buli raised the club and waited.

"In the first place, my death will profit you nothing," began the argument.

"I leave the answer to my club," was the Buli's reply.

And to every point he made the same reply, at the same time watching the missionary closely in order to forestall that cunning run-in under the lifted club. Then, and for the first time, John Starhurst knew that his death was at hand. He made no attempt to run in. Bareheaded, he stood in the sun and prayed aloud--the mysterious figure of the inevitable white man, who, with Bible, bullet, or rum bottle, has confronted the amazed savage in his every stronghold. Even so stood John Starhurst in the rock fortress of the Buli of Gatoka.

"Forgive them, for they know not what they do," he prayed. "O Lord! Have mercy upon Fiji. Have compasssion for Fiji. O Jehovah, hear us for His sake, Thy Son, whom Thou didst give that through Him all men might also become Thy children. From Thee we came, and our mind is that to Thee we may return. The land is dark, O Lord, the land is dark. But Thou art mighty to save. Reach out Thy hand, O Lord, and save Fiji, poor cannibal Fiji."

The Buli grew impatient.

"Now will I answer thee," he muttered, at the same time swinging his club with both hands.

Narau, hiding among the women and the mats, heard the impact of the blow and shuddered. Then the death song arose, and he knew his beloved missionary's body was being dragged to the oven as he heard the words:

"Drag me gently. Drag me gently."

"For I am the champion of my land."

"Give thanks! Give thanks! Give thanks!"

Next, a single voice arose out of the din, asking:

"Where is the brave man?"

A hundred voices bellowed the answer:

"Gone to be dragged into the oven and cooked."

"Where is the coward?" the single voice demanded.

"Gone to report!" the hundred voices bellowed back. "Gone to report! Gone to report!"

Narau groaned in anguish of spirit. The words of the old song were true. He was the coward, and nothing remained to him but to go and report.

[vii] http://en.wikipedia.org/wiki/Kava
[viii] http://www.faneuilhallmarketplace.com/

www.ingramcontent.com/pod-product-compliance
Ingram Content Group UK Ltd.
Pitfield, Milton Keynes, MK11 3LW, UK
UKHW041931190726
13854UKWH00004B/1542

9 781411 686496